PROVISION
AND
WEALTH

THEOLOGY OF WORK PROJECT

PROVISION
AND
WEALTH

THE BIBLE AND YOUR WORK
Study Series

HENDRICKSON
PUBLISHERS

Theology of Work
The Bible and Your Work Study Series: Provision and Wealth

© 2015 by Hendrickson Publishers Marketing, LLC
P.O. Box 3473
Peabody, Massachusetts 01961-3473

ISBN 978-1-61970-662-0

William Messenger, Executive Editor, Theology of Work Project

Sean McDonough, Biblical Editor, Theology of Work Project
Patricia Anders, Editorial Director, Hendrickson Publishers

Contributor:

Wayne Kirkland, "Provision and Wealth" Bible Study
Wayne Kirkland, "Provision & Wealth" in the *Theology of Work Bible Commentary*

The Theology of Work Project is an independent, international organization dedicated to researching, writing, and distributing materials with a biblical perspective on work. The Project's primary mission is to produce resources covering every book of the Bible plus major topics in today's workplaces. Wherever possible, the Project collaborates with other faith-and-work organizations, churches, universities and seminaries to help equip people for meaningful, productive work of every kind.

Printed in the United States of America

First Printing—May 2015

Contents

The Theology of Work

Work is not only a human calling, but also a divine one. "In the beginning God created the heavens and the earth." God worked to create us and created us to work. "The LORD God took the man and put him in the garden of Eden to till it and keep it" (Gen. 2:15). God also created work to be good, even if it's hard to see in a fallen world. To this day, God calls us to work to support ourselves and to serve others (Eph. 4:28).

Work can accomplish many of God's purposes for our lives—the basic necessities of food and shelter, as well as a sense of fulfillment and joy. Our work can create ways to help people thrive; it can discover the depths of God's creation; and it can bring us into wonderful relationships with co-workers and those who benefit from our work (customers, clients, patients, and so forth).

Yet many people face drudgery, boredom, or exploitation at work. We have bad bosses, hostile relationships, and unfriendly work environments. Our work seems useless, unappreciated, faulty, frustrating. We don't get paid enough. We get stuck in dead-end jobs or laid off or fired. We fail. Our skills become obsolete. It's a struggle just to make ends meet. But how can this be if God created work to be good—and what can we do about it? God's answers for these questions must be somewhere in the Bible, but where?

The Theology of Work Project's mission has been to study what the Bible says about work and to develop resources to apply the

Christian faith to our work. It turns out that every book of the Bible gives practical, relevant guidance that can help us do our jobs better, improve our relationships at work, support ourselves, serve others more effectively, and find meaning and value in our work. The Bible shows us how to live all of life—including work—in Christ. Only in Jesus can we and our work be transformed to become the blessing it was always meant to be.

To put it another way, if we are not following Christ during the 100,000 hours of our lives that we spend at work, are we really following Christ? Our lives are more than just one day a week at church. The fact is that God cares about our life *every day of the week*. But how do we become equipped to follow Jesus at work? In the same ways we become equipped for every aspect of life in Christ—listening to sermons, modeling our lives on others' examples, praying for God's guidance, and most of all by studying the Bible and putting it into practice.

This Theology of Work series contains a variety of books to help you apply the Scriptures and Christian faith to your work. This Bible study is one volume in the series The Bible and Your Work. It is intended for those who want to explore what the Bible says about work and how to apply it to their work in positive, practical ways. Although it can be used for individual study, Bible study is especially effective with a group of people committed to practicing what they read in Scripture. In this way, we gain from one another's perspectives and are encouraged to actually *do* what we read in Scripture. Because of the direct focus on work, The Bible and Your Work studies are especially suited for Bible studies *at* work or *with* other people in similar occupations. The following lessons are designed for thirty-minute lunch breaks (or perhaps breakfast before work) during a five-day work week.

Christians today recognize God's calling to us in and through our work—for ourselves and for those whom we serve. May God use this book to help you follow Christ in every sphere of life and work.

Will Messenger, Executive Editor
Theology of Work Project

Introduction

Mike had been weighing up the options for a week now. When he received a job offer from Tucker Consulting, he was delighted. After several months of prayer and looking for a position, it was only natural that he took this as a clear sign of real provision from God. The fact that it would pay so well and carry a lot of perks was a bonus. However, when the employment agency rang the next day and offered him a job at Create, a newly established social enterprise, he was confused. How could God be leading him to two jobs? Which one was he supposed to take?

Mike and his wife Tric had discussed the options long into the night for several days now. They kept going around in circles as they debated the pros and cons of each opportunity, and what God might be saying to them. But it was all about as clear as mud. So with a fair degree of frustration, Mike eventually rang his good mate, Chris, to get some perspective.

His friend's clarity took him by surprise. "It seems fairly obvious to me, Mike. The job with Tucker Consulting is a real opportunity and one you'd be mad to turn down. God wants to bless you. In fact, he wants the very best for you. He's giving you this job. It's staring you right between the eyeballs and I'll go so far as to say that the other offer is just a distraction from the devil!"

"But the other job has lots of opportunities to make a difference," Mike countered. "And is probably an even better fit for my skills."

"Yeah, but it's too risky financially, Mike. New company, no long-term security. How do you know it won't turn belly up within the next year like most start-ups? I just think you'd be totally irresponsible to Tric and the kids if you went this way. They deserve better—and I believe God wants you to be prosperous, not struggling."

Mike thought for a moment before responding, "Well actually, Tric is very open about the Create job. While she likes the appeal of the Tucker salary, she wonders whether the godlier thing would be to sacrifice and go for the low-paying job."

"Sorry pal, but I think that's rubbish. Sounds more like a poverty mentality to me. If you settle for less than God's blessing on your finances, I think you're not having enough faith."

 Food for Thought

What is your reaction to Chris's advice? Do you think he is right? Why or why not?

_____

_____

_____

Have you heard alternative messages to this, about provision and wealth? If so, what were they?

_____

_____

_____

God created a world in which everyone could thrive economically. In the wake of the Fall of humanity, our situations often fall short of God's original intent. Even so, God wants us to find provision (the supply of what we need) for our daily life. He also desires for us to enjoy the abundance (wealth) of his generosity. However, we live and work in a world where some live extravagantly and have enormous wealth, while many others struggle to scratch out a living, going without even the basic necessities.

Questions and concerns about God's role in our provision and wealth weigh heavily on almost every Christian's mind—whether we are rich or poor, an employee or employer, a student, parent, or retiree, a homeowner, tenant, or homeless person. Fortunately, this concern for the economic sphere of our lives is matched by the priority it is given in Scripture. Provision and wealth are far from peripheral issues in the Bible. They feature prominently through both Old and New Testaments, so we have much to draw from.

In this series of studies, we will explore what God's word has to say about:

- God's original intentions for our economic well-being.
- The effects of the Great Rebellion on our capacity to flourish.
- God's response in redeeming the economic sphere and our part in this.
- How we should treat any wealth we possess.
- What we can reasonably expect from God in regard to our provision.

Before we get started, however, here are a few items to think about:

Write down the first things that come to mind when you hear the words . . .

> *Provision:*
>
> *Wealth:*
>
> *Poverty:*

On the continuum below, estimate where you currently are, between the extremes of destitution and unbelievable wealth. (Note: Although this is a subjective exercise, where we identify ourselves will tell us much about how we read the Bible's teaching on provision and wealth.)

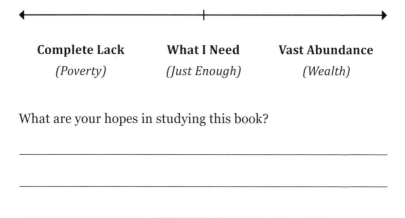

Complete Lack	**What I Need**	**Vast Abundance**
(Poverty)	*(Just Enough)*	*(Wealth)*

What are your hopes in studying this book?

_____

_____

_____

Studying the Bible is a dangerous affair. When God speaks to us through his word, he is just as likely to challenge the way we live as encourage us. When we take the text seriously, it will not leave us unchanged.

Prayer

In light of this, here's a prayer you may like to pray as you begin this series:

Lord,

We confess we are finite beings, limited in our perspective.
You are infinite and unlimited.
We are broken and sin-ridden creatures.
You are the whole and holy Creator.
We see through a glass dimly.
You see things in their completeness.
We see things as we are.
You see us, and your universe, as they really are.
So we ask for your help.
We want to hear and see you more clearly.
Break through our filtered lenses.
Open our eyes to help us see with increasing clarity your perspective, your truth, and your direction.

Amen.

Chapter 1

God's Original Intentions
(Genesis 1–2)

"In the Beginning . . ."

If we want to gain insight into God's original intentions for our provision, the best place to start is the creation narrative of Genesis 1 and 2. These two complementary passages tell us a lot about how things were meant to be. Take some time to read carefully through these two chapters. You may want to particularly note or mark any times the following words are used:

- *Bless/blessed*
- *Produce/increase*
- *Fruitful*

 Food for Thought

What is your overall impression regarding how (or in what ways) God provides for the first humans?

Air to breathe, Water to drink, plants and Fruit for food, Sunlight for warmth. God gave Mon the ability to rule over everything too.

What does the Genesis creation account specifically say about God's material provision for humankind?

Food: Fruit plants, seed-bearing plants

Water

Air

Let's focus briefly on three elements of the story: blessing, abundance, and co-creation.

Lesson #1: Blessing (Genesis 1:22, 28; 2:3)

As Genesis tells us early on in the story, "God *blessed* them." This is stated regarding both the animal life and human beings. The word *blessing*, or *bless*, is a central feature of the biblical story. It refers to God causing his creation to be fruitful and multiply.

Part of the blessing of a relationship with God is tangible, in-the-hand stuff. And these material blessings are thoroughly integrated with the other benefits of knowing and loving the Creator.

 Food for Thought

In what ways do you think Genesis is suggesting that God will bless humanity?

By God creating everything essentially
for Man and blessing both creatures
and Man and telling them to be fruitful
And multiply only makes sense that he
would bless humanity.

Make a list of all the different ways you have experienced God's blessing.

Family: BLESSED with a husband of 22 years, A wonderful son, Financially: Home, Food, Cars, Insurance, AND my family's Health

What do you think it might mean that "God blessed the seventh day" (the Sabbath)?

HE SAW All that he DID AND MADE the seventh day for rest and worshipping him. So, I think we take that Day for God and Reflect on the many blessings He has given us.

Lesson #2: Abundance (Genesis 1:11–12, 20–22, 28–30; 2:9)

The account of Genesis makes it clear that God planned for humanity to enjoy the beauty, abundance, and fruitfulness of creation. In the idyllic setting of the garden, the first humans were commanded to "be fruitful and multiply." This was a rich, fertile place, and humanity was intended to prosper in every sense. God provides an abundance of *resources* and *means* for humans to flourish.

Later in the biblical narrative, the people of Israel discover the overflowing abundance of God's provision when they finally reach the Promised Land. Deuteronomy 8:7–9 records the promise made to God's people in the desert:

> For the LORD your God is bringing you into a good land, a land with flowing streams, with springs and underground waters welling up in valleys and hills, a land of wheat and barley, of vines and fig trees and pomegranates, a land of olive trees and honey, a land where you may eat bread without scarcity, where you will lack nothing. (New Revised Standard Version)

Food for Thought

If you were to picture your current environment (perhaps the neighborhood, city, suburb, or countryside you live in) having no scarcity, where people lack nothing, what would it look like?

Fortunately for us, we live in an area (Goulesbury) where most of our neighbors are retired and seem to have what they need. I think for them, health is always the one thing in short supply

If you can, recall a time when you genuinely experienced a lack or scarcity of basic physical needs. What did it feel like? How were those needs eventually met?

When I was young, I lacked the money to fix my car, but fortunately for me my parents gave me the money

Lesson #3: Co-Creation (Genesis 1:26–28; 2:15, 19–20)

Imbedded in the Genesis story is a commission to humans to work with God in the "keeping" and development of creation. God gives people the capacity to understand the natural world so that we may use its resources. In partnership with the Creator, we are to make creative use of the resources of the earth—growing and innovating, creating new technologies and products, developing the original creation. This is sometimes referred to as the "creation mandate."

 *Food for Thought*

What role does the text suggest humans have to play in their own provision?

> We were given An Amazing gift And God wanted us to have "Ownership" of the gift so we were drawn to take care of it.

What hints are there in the story that God intends us to develop creation? He gives us so much, that even after we sin he kept providing.

> He has us name All creatures which shows us ownership and a will to take care of and develop.

At our best, we humans have cooperated with God amazingly well in developing his creation. Whether it be the development of agriculture and horticulture, the harnessing of energy, the creation of parks, gardens, and images of beauty, or the design and building of houses, appliances, clothes, and modes of transport, all such technologies that enrich our lives are expressions of co-creation with God. The capacity to innovate, produce, and develop is part of what it means to be made in God's image.

- Choose five ways humans have developed technologies that have improved our provision and wealth. Discuss the specific ways these innovations have enabled us to flourish economically.

- Are there any downsides to these innovations for humans, animals, or the natural environment?

Summary

God created a world in which everyone could thrive economically. In the wake of the Fall of humanity, our situations often fall short of God's original intent. Even so, God wants us to find provision (basic needs) for our daily life. He also desires us to enjoy the wealth (abundance) of his generosity. Furthermore, God has blessed us with a world that has ample resources to provide all we need, as well as commissioned us to work and co-create, by developing these resources for the benefit of humanity and the rest of creation.

Prayer

Spend some time expressing gratitude to God for all that he has provided and blessed us with. Be specific and don't limit it to just physical needs.

Chapter 2

The Effects of the Great Rebellion

(Genesis 3)

Lesson #1: Scavenging the Rubbish

It was a typical hot, steamy Manila afternoon. Not the kind of day you'd pick for sunbathing—at least not where I was. As I stood there, in the heart of those sprawling slums, a vast mountain of rubbish was on fire. But that was common, I was told, in the middle of the hot season. The heat had created natural combustion—enough to turn the huge scrap heap that was the Manila city dump into a mass of thick smoke. No wonder the locals called it Smokey Mountain.

It was 1986 and my wife Jill and I, along with three others, had already spent five weeks assisting a nearby mission base, feeding malnourished kids and caring for badly underdeveloped babies. I had just finished the round of the many shacks where the kids on the feeding program lived when Jeremiah, my Filipino friend and co-worker, said to me, "Come on, I want to take you somewhere."

Intrigued by his request, I began to follow him over the open sewer ditch and around the side of the mountain. The path was super-spongy—like walking on extra-padded Nikes. The ground consisted of countless thousands of tons of rubbish gradually compressing together. As we fought our way through the armies of flies that descended on anything and everything that stood still, Jeremiah said, "I want to take you up to the scavenging area."

It wasn't long before we reached the top—a place I'd never been before. Day after day I'd mixed with the people in their poor excuses for houses, chatting freely about life, sharing both laughter and pain, but never had I gone to see why 10,000 people lived on this grotesque accumulation of stinking, filthy, rotting, and disease-ridden rubbish.

As we reached the top, I looked around. Between the thick banks of wafting smoke I could see for miles into the distance. It was a great view of Manila. But the people about me weren't interested in the scenery, and I suspected Jeremiah hadn't brought me here for that reason either. I dropped my eyes, forgetting the view, and looked instead at a large group of squatters, scratching their way through the freshly dropped rubbish, searching for anything that might prove of some value for the scrap dealers.

A rubbish truck tipped its load and then chugged away, and the group scurried over to rake through the garbage with their metal hooks. Picking up wood, metal, bottles, and plastic, they dropped the scrap into large cane baskets strapped across their backs before the bulldozer came to heave the rubbish over the edge.

We stood there in silence. I turned to Jeremiah and asked him how frequently he visited this spot. "Not often," he replied. "I don't like coming here." When I asked him why not, he said, "See over there—look at those men. Do you recognize any of them?" As I looked closer I realized I knew three or four of those scavenging. They were local men I had come to know over the weeks. They all attended a Bible study group where I had assisted Jeremiah. "Have you noticed that none of them has acknowledged us? Not one of the men we know has smiled or said hello to us."

I thought about that. It made no sense. The way they were ignoring us was totally different from their normal behavior.

"You know why that is? It's because they're so ashamed to be here. They hate what they have to do for a living. It's humiliating. But they know that if they don't scavenge, their families will starve to death. They have no choice."

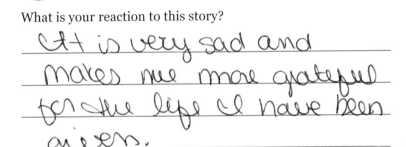 *Food for Thought*

What is your reaction to this story?

It is very sad and makes me more grateful for the life I have been given.

If God's intention was for all of humanity to thrive economically, why do more than 1.4 billion people in our world today live in extreme poverty, with a further 1.1 billion living a "hand-to-mouth" existence that is only one crisis away from disaster? What has gone wrong? Why is this the daily reality of so many people?

The fall is the obvious answer. But we as a society have turned from God and from each other.

Lesson #2: The Fall and the Curse

As you read Genesis 3, highlight the following:

- What the immediate consequence of the rebellion was;
- All the listed consequences of the rebellion; and
- The consequence that most directly affects our work and provision.

The rebellion of the first humans had a catastrophic effect on all of creation—not just their relationship with God, but also their capacity to draw provision and create wealth from the land.

At the core of this rebellion was a reshaping of *our view of God's character* and a breakdown of *our trust in him*. In *Genesis for Everyone* (WJK, 2010) theologian John Goldingay suggests that "in its shrewdness, the snake begins by making God much more restrictive and much less generous than God was. The story has emphasized the plentiful nature of God's provision and the single constraint. The snake makes it all constraint" (46).

Genesis 3:17b–19a particularly highlights the consequences for our work and provision:

> "The ground is cursed because of you. All your life you will struggle to scratch a living from it. It will grow thorns and thistles for you, though you will eat of its grains. By the sweat of your brow will you have food to eat."

 *Food for Thought*

What do you think the writer of Genesis means by the word *cursed*?

It will not be easy for him

Can you recall a time when you seriously questioned God's generosity and provision? What was it that caused you not to trust God?

When my husband was forced to make a job change. fear caused me to not trust God

What kind of factors contribute to making it a real "struggle to scratch out a living" for many people?

The cost of daycare, transportation possibly caring for an elderly parent. or illness

Think about our current economic system—a regulated market economy. What are some of the implicit assumptions it makes about provision, wealth, and God's involvement in this?

The economy basically says that the strong survives + it is our responsibility to provide for ourselves + we a successful when we are wealth

Lesson #3: Poverty—A Less-than-Perfect World

Poverty was clearly not part of God's original intention for humankind. And yet, as we have already seen, it is the reality for billions of people across the world. Poverty is often the result of a complex web of factors. For those of us who have enough, or who are wealthy, it can be easy (and convenient) to blame the people who are lacking. But to think we know why someone else is poor is simply presumptuous. Often we are not aware of what has caused this lack of provision for someone.

The fallen world is neither fair nor even-handed. None of us starts life from the same position—our family, community, and societal circumstances dictate much about our opportunities in the world.

Of course, it is true that sometimes we reap what we sow. Hard work and good choices can result in abundance, and laziness and poor choices *can* lead to poverty. We do not, however, start life on a level playing field. Some of us are fortunate to be born into loving families in prosperous circumstances, with a myriad of abilities and opportunities. Sadly, others are born into situations that are resource-less in every sense of the word. Societal factors also play a huge role in the opportunities we have. Some of us are born in to societies with access to good education, rule of law, health care, and democratic government. Others have little or no opportunity for education or good health and are stymied by corrupt economic systems and despotic governments.

And while the effects of human sin and error cause the majority of poverty, it is not necessarily *their own* sin that causes people to lack provision or wealth. A tyrant confiscates a family's land, depriving them of their capacity to produce. A factory exploits vulnerable workers by paying below legal wages. A corrupt government grants monopolies to those with political connections, shutting out everyone else. A wealthy landowner strips large tracts of forested land of vegetation, putting millions of people downstream at risk of flooding. A husband becomes addicted to gambling and leaves his wife and children penniless. Poor economic policy plunges a whole nation into stagnation and unemployment. An investment fails because of fraud and deception, leaving a family who had saved hard for the future without means.

The unpredictability of our planet also plays a part. Natural disasters—earthquakes, tsunamis, droughts, or floods—can devastate whole communities, even nations, as crops, homes, and livelihoods are destroyed in their wake. Plus, some areas of the earth seem to be much more resource-rich than others. For example, living and working on the edge of the Sahara is much more demanding than in New Zealand.

And then there are other factors that come into play—disability, illness, or aging—that don't appear to be anyone's fault, just the result of living in a less-than-perfect world. In the Old Testament three groups of people were recognized as being particularly vulnerable and powerless: the orphan (or fatherless), the widow, and the foreigner. That's why the Hebrew law and the prophets consistently implored Israel to care for these ones (see Exodus 22:22; Deuteronomy 10:18, 24:17–22; Psalm 146:9; Isaiah 1:17; Zechariah 7:9–10).

 Food for Thought

Share honestly about any assumptions you have made about people who are poor. Can you think of any experiences/conversations/literature that might have contributed to these assumptions?

When I was younger I
assumed people were poor
because the were lazy.
I believe I thought that
because my Dad always alluded
~~to that so it.~~

Think about your own neighborhood or community. If an absence of resources, powerlessness, and vulnerability are features of poverty, what type of people might be considered "poor"? What contact do you personally have with any of these individuals or groups of people?

> I think anyone that struggles to financially fulfill their and their families financial needs are poor. I do not personally have contact with any at the moment.

Summary

While there are times when the Bible connects provision or lack of it with a cause, Scripture is generally less concerned with identifying the particular causes of poverty and more concerned with the obligations of those who have wealth to care for those who lack.

Prayer

Spend some time identifying and praying for people/groups/nations for whom there is great physical need.

Chapter 3

The Dangers of Wealth

(Amos 2–5)

Lesson #1: Injustice

I was a little anxious. I was flying into Myanmar (also known as Burma) only three weeks after the bloody pro-democracy demonstrations, and I still wasn't sure it was sensible to continue with my short visit to this Asian hotspot. Even though my visa application had been miraculously granted (or so it seemed to me), I was a little nervous about what to expect. A few more tourists along with me would have eased my anxiety.

But, nonetheless, here I was. My Burmese friend met me at the airport, and his smiling face was a welcome sight. I had expected a tough interrogation at the immigration and customs desks, but it took only a few minutes to get through the officials. We left the extravagant (and nearly empty) new terminal and headed for a taxi ride into Yangon.

The next few days were a strange mix of the familiar and the disorienting. To all intents and purposes, the city looked like many another Asian metropolis, though it didn't have the in-your-face poverty and barrenness of a Kolkata or a Manila. But neither was it an affluent and immaculate Singapore. However, it *was* very green and, in a run-down kind of way, very beautiful. Stunning Buddhist pagodas (temples) dominated the skyline and the vegetation was lush.

But beneath the surface I could tell that things were not well. The stress and tension were palpable.

Trying to make sense of how this country worked was not easy. There was no banking system and cash ruled the day—either U.S. dollars or the local currency converted at exorbitant government-set exchange rates. I stayed at a fancy hotel just down the road from my hosts, feeling deeply uncomfortable with my digs. Not only were they a radical contrast to the conditions of my friends' apartment, but they were flashier than anything I'd previously stayed in, except for the hotel in Singapore on the way over. But my friend explained that it was illegal to have people to stay in homes, so a hotel or guesthouse was the only option.

To my surprise (call it naivety) I noticed that most of the guests in the hotel and restaurant were Burmese. Clearly there were some locals who were doing very well economically. Yet out on the streets it was evident that most people were barely scratching out a living. Later that day in the city, I talked to a man who was a teacher. He explained that his government pay had recently been cut and was far from sufficient for even basic survival.

Meeting me for dinner that evening, my host casually remarked that the owner of the hotel was in prison and had been for several years. Evidently he had refused to pay off the military junta with the necessary bribes and favors required to stay in business.

One day we took a taxi out of Yangon to the countryside to visit a village. The wide roads of the city were potholed and most of the houses and shacks dilapidated. But every now and then we passed flashy housing estates that wouldn't have looked out of place in Florida or Hawaii. My friend explained that they were houses for the military.

My visit to Myanmar was only a few days long. Driving back to the airport, I pondered the unfairness of it all. Here I was, free to exit this oppressive city—back to a life of liberty and ease—while my friend remained.

If there was one word that summed up my impressions of this beautiful land and its beautiful people, it was *injustice*. How could it be, I thought to myself as the plane lifted off, that the people I met had to endure such deprivation and hardship? This country, after all, was for many centuries known as "the rice bowl of South East Asia," a land rich in natural resources—rice, timber, minerals, and natural gas. Now a brutal military dictatorship ruled it with an iron fist. These officers lived in luxury, while most of their own people eked out a miserable existence.

We climbed above the cloud band. At 30,000 feet, soaring south toward home, I was reminded that just a few hundred miles to the north and east, hundreds of thousands of ethnic minority Burmese were being forced from their homes in the thick and mountainous jungle by their own country's army. Villages and crops were being pillaged and burned, and stragglers picked off for rape or forced labor. What a life.

Then God's words through the prophet Amos, written centuries before, rang in my ears:

> "Do you know what I want? I want justice—oceans of it. I want fairness—rivers of it. That's what I want. That's *all* I want." (Amos 5:24 *The Message*)

Justice, so taken for granted in my homeland, was so wretchedly absent here.

 *Food for Thought*

What is your reaction to this story?

It is very sad and unfortunate that this is still happening in todays world

Make a list of all the countries in the world where you are aware of significant issues of exploitation, oppression, injustice, corruption, or forced labor.

China   Iraq

Russia

North Korea

Iran

What about your own "world"—that is, the country, state, city, or neighborhood you live and work in? Try to make a list of situations and people where these types of issues are present.

I did a project on Sex trafficing and it is very prevelent in the United States and even MI

Lesson #2: Exploitation

It is not just national leaders who gain wealth through unjust means. Some multinational corporations exploit cheap labor markets, impose unsafe working conditions on desperate workers, or devastate local ecosystems to reap oversized profits. Then there are individuals and organizations that defraud and deceive household investors into taking excessive risks or offering high interest loans, without any concern for the people they might be hurting in the process.

This is what the Lord says:

"The people of Israel have sinned again and again,
and I will not let them go unpunished!
They sell honorable people for silver
and poor people for a pair of sandals.
They trample helpless people in the dust
and shove the oppressed out of the way." (Amos 2:6–7a)

Do what is good and run from evil
so that you may live!
Then the Lord God of Heaven's Armies will be your helper,
just as you have claimed.
Hate evil and love what is good;
turn your courts into true halls of justice.
Perhaps even yet the Lord God of Heaven's Armies
will have mercy on the remnant of his people. (Amos 5:14–15)

"I hate all your show and pretense—
the hypocrisy of your religious festivals and solemn assemblies.
I will not accept your burnt offerings and grain offerings.
I won't even notice all your choice peace offerings.
Away with your noisy hymns of praise!
I will not listen to the music of your harps.
Instead, I want to see a mighty flood of justice,
an endless river of righteous living." (Amos 5:21–24)

Read Amos 2:4–8; 3:10–4:3; 5:4–24. As you read, highlight every phrase or sentence concerning provision, wealth, economic injustice, exploitation, corruption, and violence.

 Food for Thought

What impacts you most about reading these extracts from Amos?

They will do anything
for wealth. But they
forgot God

_____

What connection does there appear to be between unjust accumulation of wealth and our worship of God?

to much unjust wealth reverse
our connection w/God.
We can not have a good
relationship with him when
we a destroying others

Lesson #3: "The Root of All Evil"

Much of the message of the prophets targets the economic injustice caused by those with wealth and power. Through spokespersons such as Amos, Micah, and Jeremiah, God states that our worship is meaningless if we are accumulating wealth through the exploitation of others.

Ensuring all members of society (and particularly the vulnerable) have access to resources in order to live a life of dignity was part of

Israel's covenantal responsibilities. Sadly, the mechanisms under the law that sought to build a fair, just, and compassionate society had been flouted and ignored. Instead of modeling God's peace and justice, Israel had become just like every other nation—a cesspit of oppression, abuse of power, and flagrant disregard for those caught on the economic scrapheap.

Of course, not all accumulation of wealth is the result of injustice. Even when it is gained through legitimate means, wealth can be harmful. Riches can cause all kinds of negative side effects. Read the following selection of verses and passages:

> But people who long to be rich fall into temptation and are trapped by many foolish and harmful desires that plunge them into ruin and destruction. For the love of money is the root of all kinds of evil. And some people, craving money, have wandered from the true faith and pierced themselves with many sorrows. (1 Timothy 6:9–10)

> Rich people may think they are wise, but a poor person with discernment can see right through them. (Proverbs 28:11)

> "Yes, your wisdom has made you very rich, and your riches have made you very proud." (Ezekiel 28:5)

> "Israel boasts, 'I am rich! I've made a fortune all by myself! No one has caught me cheating! My record is spotless!'" (Hosea 12:8)

> "But when you had eaten and were satisfied, you became proud and forgot me." (Hosea 13:6)

> "For when you have become full and prosperous and have built fine homes to live in, and when your flocks and herds have become very large and your silver and gold have multiplied along with everything else, be careful! Do not become proud at that time and forget the Lord your God, who rescued you from slavery in the land of Egypt. Do not forget that he led you through the great and terrifying wilderness with its poisonous snakes and scorpions, where it was so hot and dry. He gave you water from the rock! He

fed you with manna in the wilderness, a food unknown to your ancestors. He did this to humble you and test you for your own good. He did all this so you would never say to yourself, 'I have achieved this wealth with my own strength and energy.'" (Deuteronomy 8:12–17)

You want what you don't have, so you scheme and kill to get it. You are jealous of what others have, but you can't get it, so you fight and wage war to take it away from them. Yet you don't have what you want because you don't ask God for it. And even when you ask, you don't get it because your motives are all wrong—you want only what will give you pleasure. (James 4:2–3)

 Food for Thought

What are some of the dangers of wealth that these passages alert us to?

it will plunge you into ruin + destruction it will make you to proud + forgetted so it can lead to scheming, + killing, + jealousy

Have you observed any of these attitudes in your own life?

I sometimes find myself jealous others things.

Can you think of other dangers of having more than we need?

_We become complacent
and forget to help
& give to others._

Summary

It is too easy to think we have no need of God when our bellies are full, life is good, and the future seems assured. We can also be tempted to swallow the belief that our good fortune is solely a result of our own hard work or smarts. And the warnings against pride and arrogance, complacency, self-sufficiency, covetousness, envy, and greed should alert us to the fact that wealth is insatiable—once you have some of it, you seem to keep wanting more and more of it. If we are not careful, the desire for more will consume us; it will demand our allegiance and worship. Jesus says it bluntly:

> "No one can serve two masters. For you will hate one and love the other; you will be devoted to one and despise the other. You cannot serve both God and money." (Matthew 6:24)

Prayer

Identify three situations or groups of people in your own neighborhood, city, or nation who are suffering economically at the hands of others. Pray for them. Ask God to show you whether you might be suffering economically, either by having too little or too much. Pray about that too.

Chapter 4

Restoring the
Economic Sphere

(Colossians 1:19–22)

Lesson #1: Reconcilable Differences

While it is true that God's original intention for humanity to enjoy his provision and wealth has been disrupted, the story is not finished. God's response is to restore/redeem and put right the economic sphere so that it again provides what everyone needs.

The big picture of God's work is described by Paul in Colossians 1:19–22:

> For God in all his fullness was pleased to live in Christ, and through him God reconciled everything to himself. He made peace with everything in heaven and on earth by means of Christ's blood on the cross. This includes you who were once far away from God. You were his enemies, separated from him by your evil thoughts and actions. Yet now he has reconciled you to himself through the death of Christ in his physical body. As a result, he has brought you into his own presence, and you are holy and blameless as you stand before him without a single fault.

 *Food for Thought*

What does Paul mean by the phrase, "He made peace with every-thing"? What elements of life do you think this extends to?

I think he means God forgave everything through Jesus all elements of life we should have peace when we trust in him

The word *reconcile* is primarily a relational term. What particular relationships do you think Paul is referring to here?

He is referring to our personal relationship with him

In *The Message*, Eugene Peterson says it well in his paraphrase of these verses:

> All the broken and dislocated pieces of the universe—people and things, animals and atoms—get properly fixed and fit together in vibrant harmonies, all because of his death, his blood that poured down from the Cross.

The putting right of everything that is broken and dislocated. Rectifying, putting right, restoring, redeeming, making peace. This is what God is about.

His program for restoration is already in place. He intends to transform and redeem *everything* and *everyone*—all that he brought into being. God wants to bring order out of chaos, resolve conflict, restore relationships, and work for justice and just solutions in all situations.

In fact, God's redeeming or reconciling work involves the restoration of all four foundational relationships: with him, with ourselves, with one another, and with the rest of creation. (See Romans 8:18–23 and Ephesians 1:9–12). Restoring all of these relationships has significant economic implications.

Lesson #2: Growing and Modeling Right Attitudes

A critical way God brings about this redemption and reconciliation is through the lives of Jesus' followers. In fact, in 2 Corinthians 5:18–19 Paul states:

> All this [new life] is from God, who through Christ reconciled us to himself and gave us the ministry of reconciliation; that is, in Christ God was reconciling the world to himself, not counting their trespasses against them, and entrusting to us the message of reconciliation. (English Standard Version)

Redeeming our use of monetary resources begins with the nurturing of biblical attitudes—from which right actions will flow. Three fundamental biblical attitudes are trusteeship, gratitude, and contentment. In this chapter, we will look at trusteeship and gratitude, and we will look at contentment in chapter 5.

Trusteeship

Tom and Sue are in their mid-forties, live in what real estate agents call "a desirable home in a good suburb," and have three teenage children. Tom works for a multinational company as a senior manager and Sue is a nurse. They're involved in a church and take seriously their commitment to follow Jesus.

Nevertheless, when Tom and Sue look at their lives they feel uneasy about the ongoing pressure to earn more in order to cope with their increasing expectations of consumption. Not that their workmates or Christian friends ever think of Tom and Sue as particularly extravagant. The way they live is fairly normal within their social context.

Looking back, however, both Tom and Sue recognize that many of their choices were poor and are part of why they now have limited options. At the moment, they're in the most resource-poor period of their lives. They've discovered that raising teenagers is incredibly expensive! As Sue says, "If I'd realized the costs we'd meet at this stage of family life, I wouldn't have been so keen on shifting. Having more money for the teenage years would've taken away some of the pressure."

Tom has a similar comment:

> The problem is that even though we've always wanted to serve God, we've never really understood that our money was not just ours to do with as we pleased. Don't get me wrong. We've been faithful tithers and we've given where we could. But we've always taken it for granted that we should regularly replace our car with the latest model, or every now and then upgrade our fridge even if the old one was running okay, or get new furniture whenever we could afford it. And Sue's right. Shifting three years ago to a bigger house in a better part of town was not a good call. It just put more pressure on us financially. It gave us a bigger mortgage for one thing—and then we had to buy more furniture to fill the house! Truth is, we'd simply grown tired of our surroundings. And most of our friends were doing it, so we just assumed it was a good idea. Sue saw this really nice house across town one day, and next minute we found ourselves moving!

Sue agrees.

> Yes, it's quite ironic really. I thought having such a dream home would make our lives easier. But quite the opposite! And it's not just financially. Shifting tore us away from the people we'd been getting to know in our old suburb and church—our network of relationships. Because our lives are so hectic, with both of us

working full time and the kids involved in all kinds of activities, I regularly "buy time" by using pre-prepared foods. Plus, it isn't uncommon for us to eat out or have takeaways two or three times a week. We're on the run so much that it's the convenient thing to do.

Both Sue and Tom also agree that their loose patterns of spending have spilled over into other areas as well. Sue says:

> I'm horrified at it now. It's no wonder, looking back, that we feel we're always struggling financially—all the stuff we convinced ourselves we needed, the expensive holidays we thought we required because we were so exhausted and needed to spoil ourselves a little. Really, we've been caught in a vicious cycle—spending most of our income simply to maintain our lifestyle. If we'd dropped our expectations earlier, we would have released a lot more money for other purposes. And again, it's not just the money. It would have freed up time and energy too.

Like many of us, Tom and Sue are struggling with how to manage their resources. They genuinely want to live in a way that extracts them from the traps and dead-ends of our consumer culture, but they're not sure where to begin. It all seems just so overwhelming.

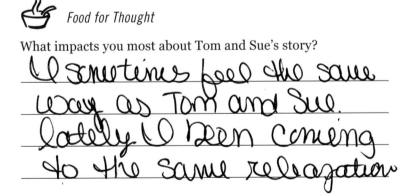 *Food for Thought*

What impacts you most about Tom and Sue's story?

I sometimes feel the same way as Tom and Sue. lately I been coming to the same realization

Are there any parts of their story that particularly resonate with you?

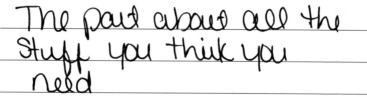

The part about all the stuff you think you need

If you were advising them, where would you suggest they begin?

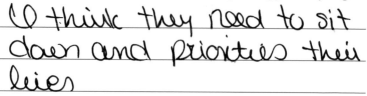

I think they need to sit down and priorities their lifes

Lesson #3: A Question of Ownership

Psalm 24:1 tells us that "the earth is the LORD's, and everything in it. The world and all its people belong to him."

As we saw in chapter 1, the first humans were directed by God to take care of the garden. They were to view themselves as caretakers of the created order. Acting as trustees of whatever wealth we have been given is foundational to a biblical perspective on provision and wealth. These resources are not for us to do with as we please—as Jesus' well-known parable of the three servants, or talents, in Matthew 25:14–30 reminds us:

> "Again, the Kingdom of Heaven can be illustrated by the story of a man going on a long trip. He called together his servants and entrusted his money to them while he was gone. He gave five bags of silver to one, two bags of silver to another, and one bag of silver to the last—dividing it in proportion to their abilities. He then left on his trip.

"The servant who received the five bags of silver began to invest the money and earned five more. The servant with two bags of silver also went to work and earned two more. But the servant who received the one bag of silver dug a hole in the ground and hid the master's money.

"After a long time their master returned from his trip and called them to give an account of how they had used his money. The servant to whom he had entrusted the five bags of silver came forward with five more and said, 'Master, you gave me five bags of silver to invest, and I have earned five more.'

"The master was full of praise. 'Well done, my good and faithful servant. You have been faithful in handling this small amount, so now I will give you many more responsibilities. Let's celebrate together!'

. . . "Then the servant with the one bag of silver came and said, 'Master, I knew you were a harsh man, harvesting crops you didn't plant and gathering crops you didn't cultivate. I was afraid I would lose your money, so I hid it in the earth. Look, here is your money back.'

"But the master replied, 'You wicked and lazy servant! If you knew I harvested crops I didn't plant and gathered crops I didn't cultivate, why didn't you deposit my money in the bank? At least I could have gotten some interest on it.'

"Then he ordered, 'Take the money from this servant, and give it to the one with the ten bags of silver. To those who use well what they are given, even more will be given, and they will have an abundance. But from those who do nothing, even what little they have will be taken away. Now throw this useless servant into outer darkness, where there will be weeping and gnashing of teeth.'"

And from Luke:

"When someone has been given much, much will be required in return; and when someone has been entrusted with much, even more will be required." (12:48b)

Food for Thought

Who, specifically, might Jesus be referring to when he talks about the "wicked and lazy servant"? Why would they be considered this?

Because they didn't want to try to do anything w/ what he was given

What kinds of resources—apart from just money—has God entrusted us with?

He has given us each talents that he expects us to use.

What other words are sometimes used to describe our role as trustees or servants?

helper, dependant, guardian, keeper

In *Mere Christianity*, C. S. Lewis writes, "Does it not make a great difference whether I am, so to speak, the landlord of my own mind and body, or only a tenant, responsible to the real landlord?" Discuss.

We are a tenant, God has given us this body to do great things

Why do you think we're so often tempted to treat what we have been given as our own? What particular resources do you find the hardest to consider yourself a trustee of and not an owner? Why?

We get complacent. All my possessions but especially my son. Because it feels as if since I gave birth to him he belongs to me.

Summary

What we have been given (our money, time, abilities, and other resources) are not our own. God is the owner. We are the trustees. Our role is to employ the resources entrusted to us in God's work of restoration.

A Trustee's Prayer

Lord,

We remind ourselves today that all we have is yours, not our own.

So help us to manage your gift of time well.

Help us to invest your gift of money and possessions wisely.

May the unique personality, skills, experiences, and abilities entrusted to each of us be well nurtured, developed, and used for your purposes.

May we appreciate the gift of the loved ones you've placed around us.

All of creation is a gift to be stewarded.

Let us be your servants this day—not abusing or misusing, always treating with care.

Lord, help us to know what to do with what you've given us,

that you may be glorified and your kingdom built.

In the name of the supreme example of trustees, Jesus.

Amen.

Chapter 5

Gratitude and Contentment
(1 Corinthians 4:7 and Philippians 4:11–19)

Lesson #1: Out of Grace, Gratitude

Victor Hugo is one of the great French novelists. In 1862 he wrote *Les Miserables*, which in English means "the wretched or poor ones." The novel is set in the early part of the nineteenth century in France in a time when life was dreadful for a large proportion of the population.

Reentering this world for the first time in nineteen years is Jean Valjean, Hugo's central character. The year is 1815 and Valjean has just been released from prison on parole. As the story progresses, we discover he was originally arrested for stealing a loaf of bread as a last resort to feed his family. His initial term was for five years but was progressively extended for several escape attempts.

The hard labor of Toulon prison has taken the best years of Jean Valjean's life, but he remains a strong and fit man in midlife. However, he quickly discovers that re-establishing a meaningful life for himself on the outside is nigh impossible. At all times he must carry the yellow "ticket-of-leave" (passport) wherever he goes. By law he must present this to potential employers and landlords. Marked forever as a convict, Valjean is trapped and condemned to be an outcast in his own country. No one wants to know him. No one wants to hire him. No innkeeper will even let him stay at his inn.

So in desperation late one night Jean Valjean knocks on the door of the bishop of Digne. Much to his surprise, the bishop invites him in, feeds him, and offers him a bed. Embittered by years of hardship, however, Valjean repays the bishop's kindness by stealing his silver and leaving in the middle of the night. Caught by the gendarmes (police) a few hours later, the paroled convict is brought in chains before the bishop. The police expect to be congratulated by the bishop for recovering his stolen silver. Instead, something remarkable happens. Much to everyone's consternation, the bishop lies to the gendarmes in order to save Valjean from life imprisonment. He tells them that he has given Valjean the silver and is only angry at him because he failed to also take the silver candlesticks as the bishop had instructed him to!

Valjean is overcome. This supreme act of grace causes him to turn his life around. He is blindsided by the inexplicable generosity of the bishop. The rest of the story hinges on this one watershed event. Several years later, we discover Valjean has established himself as a successful businessman and is living under the pseudonym of Monsieur Madeleine.

There are many more twists and turns to his story, but it quickly becomes clear that the remarkable act of grace by the bishop has thoroughly transformed Jean Valjean. In deep gratitude he has committed himself to a life of serving God and others.

 Food for Thought

Why do you think the bishop took pity on Valjean? Why would he give him the candlesticks as well? How does this tie into what Jesus says in Luke 6:27–36?

_____

_____

_____

Why do you think Jean Valjean was able to make gratitude such a core element of his life?

_____

_____

_____

Lesson #2: Living in Gratitude

If we understand that everything we have is God's—including our capacity to work, engage in business, create and produce, and sell and build wealth—we will be grateful to God. In fact, gratitude is our first and foundational response to God's grace and provision. And its practice has the potential to change the way we view and treat our material possessions.

In contrast, it's easy to buy into a culture of ingratitude and entitlement—which encourages us to believe that what we have is mainly a result of our own hard work and genius, or that we are somehow "owed" something. This betrays an inflated view of our importance and a limited awareness of gift, grace, and good fortune in our lives.

We need to remember—and live out each day—Paul's words to the church in Corinth:

> What do you have that God hasn't given you? And if everything you have is from God, why boast as though it were not a gift? (1 Corinthians 4:7)

Food for Thought

What is Paul's fundamental assumption in 1 Corinthians 4:7?

_____

_____

_____

Why is often so difficult to cultivate genuine gratitude for what we have?

_____

_____

_____

What role do you think envy (the craving of what others have) plays in our ingratitude?

_____

_____

What are some ways we can become more thankful for what we do have?

_____

_____

Make a list of all the things for which you can be grateful to God and to others. Spend some time reflecting on these.

_____

_____

Lesson #3: "The Secret of Living in Every Situation"

As we know from Luke's recorded events in Acts and Paul's various letters to the churches, the Apostle Paul suffered quite a bit in the name of Jesus. Here is a summary from Paul himself in 2 Corinthians 6:5–10.

> We have been beaten, been put in prison, faced angry mobs, worked to exhaustion, endured sleepless nights, and gone without food. We prove ourselves by our purity, our understanding, our patience, our kindness, by the Holy Spirit within us, and by our sincere love. We faithfully preach the truth. God's power is working in us. We use the weapons of righteousness in the right hand for attack and the left hand for defense. We serve God whether people honor us or despise us, whether they slander us or praise us. We are honest, but they call us impostors. We are ignored, even though we are well known. We live close to death, but we are still alive. We have been beaten, but we have not been killed. Our hearts ache, but we always have joy. We are poor, but we give spiritual riches to others. We own nothing, and yet we have everything.

He could complain, but he doesn't. In fact, he says he is actually content despite his sufferings and deprivations!

> Not that I was ever in need, for I have learned how to be content with whatever I have. I know how to live on almost nothing or with everything. I have learned the secret of living in every situation, whether it is with a full stomach or empty, with plenty or little. For I can do everything through Christ, who gives me strength. . . . At the moment I have all I need—and more! I am generously supplied with the gifts you sent me. . . . And this same God who takes care of me will supply all your needs from his glorious riches, which have been given to us in Christ Jesus. (Philippians 4:11–13, 18–19)

Food for Thought

What particular word, phrase, or thought most impacts you from the above passages?

When Paul writes about "need," what kind of things do you think he might be referring to?

Paul says that he has learned to be content with whatever he has. Share any thoughts you have about how he might have learned this.

Earlier in chapter 4 of his letter to the Philippians, Paul encourages them: "Don't worry about anything; instead, pray about everything. Tell God what you need, and thank him for all he has done" (4:6). What role does worry and anxiety often play in our economic discontent?

What are some of the cultural and media messages we come into contact with that work against developing contentment?

_____

_____

_____

What are some ways we might be able to determine what is enough (pay, savings, profit, possessions, hours worked, house size, and so forth)?

_____

_____

_____

Summary

Trusteeship. Gratitude. Contentment. These three biblical attitudes lay the foundation for us to work with God to restore the economic sphere. In *The Irresistible Revolution: Living as an Ordinary Radical* (Zondervan, 2006), author/activist Shane Claibourne suggests:

> We need a third way; neither the prosperity gospel nor the poverty gospel, but the gospel of abundance rooted in a theology of enough. . . . After seeing plenty of poor folks forced into economic crimes by their poverty and after seeing plenty of rich folks so content in their riches that they forget they need God or anyone else, I think we are all ready for something new. (126)

Prayer

Look back at the list you made in this study of things you are grateful for. Spend some time voicing your gratitude to God for them.

Chapter 6

Changing Our Personal Lifestyles

(Acts 2:42–47 and Luke 14:1–14)

Lesson #1: "All Things in Common"

The biblical attitudes of trusteeship, gratitude, and contentment will inevitably lead to change in our personal lifestyles. This was certainly the experience of the first Christians. In the days immediately following Pentecost, a lot was happening. Luke gives us a brief glimpse of these heady days:

> And they continued steadfastly in the apostles' doctrine and fellowship, in the breaking of bread, and in prayers. Then fear came upon every soul, and many wonders and signs were done through the apostles. Now all who believed were together, and had all things in common, and sold their possessions and goods, and divided them among all, as anyone had need. So continuing daily with one accord in the temple, and breaking bread from house to house, they ate their food with gladness and simplicity of heart, praising God and having favor with all the people. And the Lord added to the church daily those who were being saved. (Acts 2:42–47 New King James Version)

> Now the multitude of those who believed were of one heart and one soul; neither did anyone say that any of the things he possessed was his own, but they had all things in common. And with great power the apostles gave witness to the resurrection of the Lord Jesus. And great grace was upon them all. Nor was there anyone among them who lacked; for all who were possessors of lands or houses sold them, and brought the proceeds of the things that were sold, and

laid them at the apostles' feet; and they distributed to each as anyone had need. (Acts 4:32–35 NKJV)

One of the more frequent words translated as "community" or "fellowship" in the New Testament is *koinonia*. The Apostle Paul is particularly fond of using it, but here in Acts 2 Luke employs this word to help describe what is going on.

Luke clearly means much more than sharing in a cup of coffee after a church service. *Koinonia* emphasizes *active participation together*—owning a share in something rather than just being associated with it. A strong sense of partnership. As we read Luke's description we can see that this spills over into the economic. *Koinonia* definitely has financial implications.

Most scholars believe that having "all things in common" was an example of individuals selling excess property rather than absolute collectivism. But even so, this is a remarkable display of the sharing of resources. And it is a reminder that God's vision of provision and wealth is for them to be communal rather than just individual matters.

 Food for Thought

When you've heard the word *fellowship* (or *koinonia*) used, how has it usually been understood?

_____

_____

What appear to be the key characteristics of the shared life for the church in Jerusalem?

_____

_____

Do you know of Christian communities/churches that practice some form of sharing of resources? If so, how have they gone about it?

_____

_____

What do you think some of the challenges and difficulties of sharing financial resources in a faith community might be?

_____

_____

What personal experience have you had of the sharing of resources in a faith community?

_____

_____

Lesson #2: Personal Engagement

In Luke 14, Jesus accepts a Sabbath dinner invitation to the home of a leader of the Pharisees. After healing a man at the dinner and asking questions that the other guests dare not answer, Jesus notices how these same guests were trying to sit as close as possible to the honored head of the table. He then uses this opportunity to teach them a lesson in humility about taking the lowest seat: "For those who exalt themselves will be humbled, and those who humble themselves will be exalted" (14:11).

Luke continues the story:

> Then he turned to his host. "When you put on a luncheon or a banquet," he said, "don't invite your friends, brothers, relatives, and rich neighbors. For they will invite you back, and that will be

your only reward. Instead, invite the poor, the crippled, the lame, and the blind. Then at the resurrection of the righteous, God will reward you for inviting those who could not repay you." (14:12–14)

 Food for Thought

What kinds of people might be the equivalent today (in your community) of "the poor, the crippled, the lame, and the blind"?

_____

_____

What are some of the challenges for you in offering hospitality to these people?

_____

_____

Why does Jesus indicate that we will be blessed by practicing this form of hospitality?

_____

_____

Can you think of other parables of Jesus that echo similar challenges?

_____

_____

In what ways did Jesus model this in his own life and ministry? (Be as specific as you can, recalling particular examples.)

_____

_____

Lesson #3: Christian Hospitality

One of the key Greek words translated into hospitality is *philo-xenia*, which literally means "the love of the stranger." This is what makes the giving of hospitality distinctively "Christian"—it is welcoming those we normally wouldn't relate to, and not doing so on the basis of reciprocal benefits.

Just like the Israelites, who were commanded to care for those most vulnerable in their society—the orphans, widows, and foreigners—the first followers of Jesus understood the call to go beyond the comfort of their own family and friends and care for those on the margins.

This is a call to more than just financial giving and sharing of resources. It involves the personal engagement and building of relationship with the "stranger"—the person who is often excluded from "the party." When those who have much get to know those who have little, amazing things can happen: perspectives and stereotypes change and both parties discover that they have much in common, as well as much to learn from each other.

Part of the challenge in our society today is the significant social distance there often is between the "haves" and the "have-nots." For many people in well-paying jobs, living in well-to-do neighborhoods, mixing in affluent friendship groups, and worshipping in prosperous churches, connecting with the poor is not likely to be a part of everyday life. Building personal relationships will require intentionally moving out of accustomed circles and into uncomfortable situations. It may even require relocation. And if it is to be genuine Christian hospitality, it will need to avoid paternalism (which disempowers others by doing for them what they can do for themselves) and seek to minimize power imbalances.

Clapham—An Example of Community and Personal Engagement

The 2006 movie *Amazing Grace* tells the story of William Wilberforce, the British Member of Parliament who spearheaded the movement to abolish the English slave trade (and eventually slavery itself) in the late eighteenth and early nineteenth centuries.

In the late 1780s, much of the wealth of the British Empire was dependent on the trading of slaves from West Africa across to the New World. In fact, it would not be overstating matters to say that the growing power of "Great" Britain occurred on the backs of slaves. Challenging this immoral trade inevitably pitted the proponents of abolition against enormous and powerful economic interests. This helps to explain why the anti-slavery movement had to battle for decades before they succeeded in stopping it.

It was not until 1807 (a full twenty years after the campaign began) that the slave trade was abolished, and then a further twenty-six years until slavery itself was made illegal. Appealing to politicians, who were themselves profiting significantly from the trade (either directly or indirectly) or were backed by the barons of industry, required more than just pointing out the immorality of such treatment. For the truth is that so often when we think our livelihood is threatened, any ethical concerns are relegated to the too-hard basket. Money does indeed rule.

The movie paints well this long battle—as it does the forces of opposition, abuse, and ridicule the abolitionists had to endure. What is less obvious, however, is that Wilberforce was one of a group of men and women working together to bring change. He was not acting alone. Nor was he the only leader. Wilberforce was really just the most public face of a community of people who came to be known later as the Clapham Sect. It was this group of remarkable individuals and families who were the nerve center of the anti-slave trade and anti-slavery campaigns.

It began in the Village of Clapham, on the edge of London, where a banker named Henry Thornton lived with his family. It was the Thorntons who invited young MP William Wilberforce to move there in the late 1780s. Soon Thornton had gathered together others of like mind, who shared a passion for taking their evangelical faith boldly into the world of English society. Many in this group came to live in Clapham—such as John Venn (the vicar of the local parish), lawyer James Stephen, long-time campaigner Granville Sharp, gifted researcher and writer Thomas Clarkson, and the former governor-general of India, Lord Teignmouth. Then there was Zachary Macaulay, a fellow of the Royal Society whose brilliant mind was applied to preparing evidence and reasoned arguments. (When the group needed an answer to a question, Wilberforce would sometimes joke, "Let's look it up in Macaulay.") Other members of the community lived at some distance, but were still relationally connected and committed to the group's endeavors—people such as the writer Hannah More, influential clergyman Charles Simeon, and the president of Queens College, Cambridge, Isaac Milner.

The Claphamites were not a clearly delineated group. Nor would they have viewed themselves as anything more than evangelical Anglicans with a passion for "Christianity in action." Nevertheless, at its core, Clapham became a vibrant center of community, with families living in each other's homes, daily prayers, and collaborative projects developed over the kitchen table and in Thornton's library. In today's terminology they might be described as a "missional community."

While the slave trade campaign was the core issue at the heart of the Clapham Sect's mission, they spearheaded numerous other attempts to bring transformation. Their political conservatism was sometimes criticized—particularly because of their reluctance to support increased democratic rights, trade unions, or anything else that might undermine the social order of their society. Nevertheless, the group was passionate about many of the great injustices of the day, initiating campaigns for penal reform, the abolition of the press gang, relief of chimney boys, education for all, and the regulation of factory conditions—which in their day were appalling. They established numerous organizations ("voluntary societies") to assist and relieve the poor. Additionally, they fought to stop indecent literature, abolish the lottery and the cruel animal sports of the day, and to promote the Sabbath as a day of rest. To give some idea of the breadth of their interests, William Wilberforce was a member of no less than sixty-nine of these voluntary societies!

Claphamites were also key initiators in the founding of the Church Missionary Society (CMS), the British and Foreign Bible Society, and the Sunday school movement, as well as the creation of Sierra Leone as a colony in West Africa for freed slaves.

Viewing themselves as trustees of the resources God had given them, the men and women of Clapham strategically pooled their time, abilities, spheres of influence, and money to the causes they gave themselves to. They worked at the political level agitating for change and using their organizational and writing skills to mobilize public opinion. And they gave their considerable financial resources to fund numerous causes. Macaulay is reputed to have given away all of his vast fortune, dying a poor man. Wilberforce's "generosity was warm-hearted and impetuous," while Thornton was more calculating and planned but no less generous (Robin Furneaux, *William Wilberforce* [Hamish Hamilton, 1974]).

Though we live in different times, Clapham is a powerful example. It shows how a community of privilege and wealth was able to apply their resources to the pursuit of a vision.

Food for Thought

Share your reactions to the Clapham story.

_____

_____

_____

_____

What in particular do you think you can learn from their experience?

_____

_____

_____

_____

Summary

When our lives are full of gratitude and contentment, and we take seriously our roles as trustees of our resources, our personal lifestyles can't help but change. We will seek to live more communally and become personally engaged with those in need. The call to both community and personal engagement are a response to the generous hospitality of the Trinity—Father, Son, and Holy Spirit—who welcome us into their life and mission.

Prayer and Communion

If it is appropriate in your tradition, take time to break bread together. As you do, you may like to pray this prayer:

Father, Son, and Holy Spirit,

We come to your table now. Thank you for your gracious invitation to join in this meal. For here you model to us the heart of hospitality. Though we have little to bring—apart from our presence—still you welcome us with grace and generosity. May we in turn welcome one another in the same spirit.

We recognize that you are not only our host but also our meal. So we eat and drink with and of you. May this bread and wine be sustenance for the journey, bringing forgiveness, cleansing, healing, and empowerment so that we find our very lives in you.

We ask this in the name of Jesus—the one whose costly sacrifice made this meal possible.

Amen.

Chapter 7

Aiding Those in Poverty
(2 Corinthians 8–9)

In the eighteenth century a substantial revival occurred across Great Britain. Thousands of working class poor came to faith—people for whom the church had been a closed door and completely alien environment. One of the leaders of this Great Awakening was John Wesley, an Oxford-educated Anglican priest.

When churches barred him from preaching his messages of new birth, he took to the fields and streets. This was a brilliant move. Most of his audience would never have been accepted and welcomed in the churches, and so he figured that if the churches wouldn't let the poor come to them, then he would go to the poor. As Wesley himself put it, "I look upon all the world as my parish."

Part of John Wesley's genius was his vision and ability to organize the growing numbers of the poor who were coming to Christ into small communities (called "bands" and "classes") where they began to be transformed by the gospel. These small groups were greenhouses for change. It was in these mini-communities that people who previously were completely ignorant of the gospel began to discover and work out a discipleship that transformed every area of their lives. As a result, some significant social and economic changes occurred in the fabric of British society.

Their growing faith established a strong work ethic and a freeing from addictions such as alcohol and gambling. This made economic mobility almost inevitable. As they worked harder and stopped spending their money on reckless and wasteful pursuits, families discovered they were able to save and improve their physical circumstances quite dramatically. Their thrift and work lifted substantial numbers of them out of poverty and into a burgeoning middle class.

One could easily assume that John Wesley would have been well pleased with this upward mobility. After all, it showed that faith was making a demonstrative difference in people's day-to-day living. And to a degree he was.

Wesley, however, became increasingly disturbed. He noticed that with such upward mobility his young converts' passion for radical discipleship mellowed. Comfortable complacency frequently took root, and the zeal they once had to live passionate, selfless lives of risk and faith drained away.

His disciples' growing affluence began to undermine the vigor of their discipleship.

In contrast to many of his converts, John Wesley's approach to money was summed up in his statement: "Earn all you can; give all you can; save all you can." This was his maxim. By "save all you can," he meant "spend as little on yourself as you can," as we would put it in today's idiom. And being the highly disciplined and organized person he was, he lived it out right through his life. In spite of the fact that his income increased dramatically through his fifty-plus years of itinerant preaching and organizing (mainly because of the royalties from material he authored), Wesley's lifestyle changed little. By the time of his death, he was still living on little more than he had been decades earlier. He gave away virtually all his earnings and died with little left over.

Food for Thought

Share something that impacts you from this story.

_____

_____

_____

Discuss John Wesley's conundrum. How can we stay hungry for God, while having more than enough for living?

_____

_____

_____

What about Wesley's maxim? In what ways do you agree or disagree with it?

_____

_____

_____

Lesson #1: Giving

Many discussions about giving in the Bible begin with the tithe (literally, "tenth"). This is understandable. It forms the cornerstone of the Jewish law's commands on giving. However, what is often neglected in these discussions is that there were multiple tithes mandated (two or three, in fact). Furthermore, when it comes to the New Testament, tithing is barely mentioned, and when it is, it is largely framed in the negative, as in Luke 11:42 and 18:18–30 or Hebrews 7.

A fair question to ask is why? It is reasonable to assume that while tithing was not actively discouraged among the early Jewish believers, it is largely superseded in the new covenant by the greater principle of generosity. People are encouraged to give freely and according to their means.

The biggest single block of writing in the New Testament about giving is found in Paul's second letter to the church at Corinth. It's a good place to base ourselves as we seek to understand the Bible's approach.

 Food for Thought

Read 2 Corinthians 8–9. What impacts you most about what Paul is saying here?

_____

_____

_____

In 8:9 Paul says, "You know the generous grace of our Lord Jesus Christ. Though he was rich, yet for your sakes he became poor, so that by his poverty he could make you rich." What do you think is Paul's main point here?

_____

_____

Make a brief list of the key principles around giving that Paul articulates in this passage.

_____

_____

Discuss what application/s they might have to your particular context.

_____

_____

_____

_____

Paul's line of thought suggests that whatever resources we possess are intended to bless the community around us, even if using "our" resources for others requires significant sacrifice. Like Jesus, we are called in some sense to become poor so that we can make others rich. This is immensely challenging to most Christians in the West, whose wealth far exceeds that of Christians in most of the world who struggle to survive on a day-to-day basis.

"Becoming poor" as Jesus did has many meanings besides losing all our stuff. But giving away some significant amount of wealth is surely included in what Paul meant by becoming poor. It is not easy to give generously. It is personally counterintuitive and deeply countercultural. On a personal level, we fear that if we give generously, then we won't have enough for our own needs. Elements of our culture reinforce this fear by presenting ever-increasing "needs" to us, and by appealing to our desire to find security by owning and hoarding.

Of course, having determined to give, we need to answer questions of _where_ and _how_. Wisdom is required to discern the most helpful and appropriate of a myriad of options. For not all giving expresses wise trusteeship. In fact, sadly, some giving may actually even hurt the very people it seeks to help.

Food for Thought

What might be reasons why we don't give more than we do?

_____

_____

_____

Which (if any) of these reasons have some validity? Why?

_____

_____

_____

Many of our giving choices are not either/or's; they span a continuum. Here are some of the options:

> Organizations . . . . Individuals
>
> Local . . . . Overseas
>
> Relief (handout) . . . . Development (hand-up)
>
> Social justice . . . . Evangelism
>
> Cross-cultural missionaries. . . . Indigenous missionaries
>
> Partnership . . . . Donor

Discuss how you determine where to give. What are some of the issues involved?

_____

_____

_____

What kinds of guiding principles do you think would be important in determining who and what to give to?

_____

_____

_____

Lesson #2: Investing

Giving financially is not the only way to aid those who are struggling economically. Wise investment of wealth can also be effective in helping the poor. In recent decades, two broad movements illustrate what can be achieved by investing in poor communities and those who struggle to make ends meet.

The first is the world of *microfinance*. Across the globe, though particularly in developing nations, cooperatives are established in poor communities to make loans to initiate small businesses. As these small enterprises generate income, the start-up loan is paid back and the capital lent to new small businesses. At least, that is the intention. The effectiveness of microfinance seems to be uneven in various contexts, and it has its share of supporters and critics. At its best, it is a mechanism for those with entrepreneurial abilities to obtain capital, create a value-adding business, provide for themselves, and benefit their communities. It is far from perfect, however, and has some significant challenges to overcome.

Another broad form of microfinance is that of "savings-led" cooperatives, which rather than giving loans to members asks them to commit to saving a small amount per week (as little as a cup of rice). This is then aggregated with the rest of the group and eventually invested. Over time, with support and mentoring, the cooperative builds a reservoir of capital, which can be drawn on by individuals for urgent needs or borrowed in order to begin a business. Savings-led cooperatives help poor communities overcome one of the primary barriers for people improving their lot—a lack of options for safely investing their miniscule savings.

The second movement, which is rapidly growing in momentum in both developed and developing nations, is that of *social enterprise*. These businesses are established to achieve social goals, in addition to being profitable. Such enterprises often seek to generate a "sustainable" profit, but not necessarily to maximize return on investment. Many social enterprises employ those who would otherwise struggle to find work: homeless or semi-homeless people, refugees, those who have been in prison, people with physical disabilities or mental health issues, women seeking to escape prostitution, and those struggling with addictions. Other enterprises focus on social or environmental issues, seeking to improve the well-being of communities and the environment. Whether through recycling, social housing, health services for those who struggle, or teaching sustainable food practices, such businesses can make a huge difference to the quality of life.

Both microfinance and social enterprises take the "hand-up" approach to aiding those trapped in poverty. At their best, they empower and give people dignity by helping provide the means by which they can help themselves. Investing in such enterprises can make a big difference to the provision and wealth of whole communities.

 *Food for Thought*

What do you think might be some of the merits and potential pitfalls of these two main forms of microfinance?

_____

_____

_____

_____

Read the parable of the vineyard workers in Matthew 20:1–16. In particular, reflect on verses 6–7. What do these workers say is the reason they haven't been working? What do you think might have been the reason/s for this? Discuss whether the vineyard owner's business might be viewed in some way as a social enterprise?

_____

_____

_____

_____

Do you know of any social enterprise functioning in your community or city? What is its primary goal/s? Who does it seek to employ and/or channel its profit to?

_____

_____

_____

_____

Lesson #3: Spending

A third way we can aid the poor is by ethical consumption. It may seem odd to suggest that we can help by *spending*—after all, we often associate spending with excessive consumption. Of course, there's virtue in reducing our consumption by not buying things we don't need. With stuff we *do* require, however, spending more for the items we consume may improve the lives of those who grow, make, or sell them.

In the present global economy, many workers are paid too little to provide for their daily needs, while those who purchase the goods and services they contribute could easily afford to pay a higher price. If there was a way for consumers to pay more—and for that increase to go to the workers who need it—spending could actually help aid poor people.

The fair trade and ethical consumption movements have been growing exponentially over the past few decades. They seek to provide ways for those in the developed world to pay fair prices for products made in the developing world. For example, fair trade looks to compensate small coffee, tea, cocoa, sugar, and cotton growers, craft makers, and other small industries equitably for their work. Ethical consumption also considers the environmental practices of sourcing raw material and manufacturing. One such example is timber and furniture from sustainable forests.

 Food for Thought

Share your own experience of buying fair trade and/or environmentally sustainable products.

_____

_____

_____

The fair trade movement covers only a small number of products sourced or manufactured in the developing world. Share your thoughts and ideas on how you might be more discerning in determining which companies to buy from when it comes to non-fair trade products.

_____

_____

_____

_____

Summary

Giving. Investing. Spending. All of these activities can be undertaken wisely and generously, in order to aid those unable to provide enough for themselves and their families. For those of us with excess, the Bible consistently commands us to do so judiciously. As Jesus himself said in Matthew 10:8, "Give as freely as you have received!"

Prayer

Share a struggle you have regarding giving, investing, or spending. Pray for one another.

Chapter 8

Contrasting Responses
(Luke 16 and Nehemiah 5)

The Bible includes many examples of wealthy people who say they follow God. Here are two characters who offer contrasting responses to those in need. We can learn from both.

Lesson #1: Parable of the Rich Man and Lazarus

The parable of the rich man and Lazarus in Luke 16:19–31 is one of the most disturbing of Jesus' stories—at least for those of us who have more than we need. In Luke's recollection of this parable, it appears that Jesus is taking a well-known folktale in the ancient world—about the reversal that would happen in the future life—and putting his own spin on it.

One of the beliefs most Jews in Jesus' day carried was that wealth was a clear sign of God's blessing and approval, while poverty was a sign of God's disapproval. The Pharisees (who are represented by the rich man in this parable) certainly believed this was the case. Their relative wealth was "proof" that they were righteous. No wonder, then, that the rich man's attitude to Lazarus was so arrogant and superior—even during his precarious after-death situation! Like most of Jesus' audience, the rich man would have believed that Lazarus's earthly state was a result of his own sin and bad choices.

Of course, many of the most revered characters in the Old Testament were wealthy—people such as Abraham, Boaz, Job, and Solomon. While there is little doubt their experience of abundance was in some way tied to their faithfulness to God, a strong connection between righteousness and wealth is difficult to make. The story of the people of Israel confirms this assessment. Many wealthy people in the Bible prosper because of their *wickedness*, not their righteousness.

The association between righteousness and wealth is even more tenuous in the New Testament. In fact, biblical scholar Gordon Fee argues that wealth is *never* related to a life of obedience in the Gospels and other New Testament books. Neither is poverty an indication of God's disapproval or punishment.

In his encounter with the rich young ruler (Matthew 19), Jesus comments that it is easier for a camel to pass through the eye of a needle than for a rich man to enter the kingdom. The shock of this statement causes his disciples to ask, "Then who can be saved?" In other words, "If not a rich man, then surely there's no hope for anyone else?" Like the Pharisees, the disciples reflected the common view of the day. But Jesus was unequivocal: wealth is not a sign of righteousness; in fact, it can be a grave peril to our relationship with God.

 Food for Thought

Who do you think Jesus is suggesting "the rich man" is representative of? (For a clue, read the few verses before the parable.)

_____

_____

_____

What are some of the characteristics of this group of people, according to Luke 16:19–20?

_____

_____

What does the story tell us about the rich man's proximity to Lazarus?

Geographically:_____

_____

_____

Socially:_____

_____

_____

Economically:_____

_____

_____

How did the rich man relate to or treat Lazarus?

In this life:_____

_____

_____

After death:_____

_____

_____

What might this all suggest about the rich man's view of why Lazarus was poor and why he himself was rich?

_____

_____

_____

Lesson #2: Nehemiah's Example

In contrast to the Pharisees, the Old Testament character Nehemiah chose quite a different response to the needs of his day.

Nehemiah was the governor of the city of Jerusalem, working as a delegated leader for a foreign government, Persia. A significant aspect of his work was to oversee the rebuilding of the city walls.

As a high-level public servant, Nehemiah was well rewarded materially. It would have been easy for him to just enjoy the privileges that went with his position. Instead, he made deliberate choices to use his influence and wealth so that he could (in the words of the prophet Micah) "act justly and love mercy."

> When I heard their complaints, I was very angry. After thinking it over, I spoke out against these nobles and officials. I told them, "You are hurting your own relatives by charging interest when they borrow money!" Then I called a public meeting to deal with the problem.
>
> At the meeting I said to them, "We are doing all we can to redeem our Jewish relatives who have had to sell themselves to pagan foreigners, but you are selling them back into slavery again. How often must we redeem them?" And they had nothing to say in their defense.
>
> Then I pressed further, "What you are doing is not right! Should you not walk in the fear of our God in order to avoid being mocked

by enemy nations? I myself, as well as my brothers and my workers, have been lending the people money and grain, but now let
us stop this business of charging interest. You must restore their
fields, vineyards, olive groves, and homes to them this very day.
And repay the interest you charged when you lent them money,
grain, new wine, and olive oil." (Nehemiah 5:6–11)

 Food for Thought

Read Nehemiah 5 in its entirety. What were the specific issues of
injustice, exploitation, and inequity that made Nehemiah so angry?

_____

_____

_____

From what you understand about the Jewish law, how was it being
flouted?

_____

_____

_____

In what ways did Nehemiah seek to alleviate poverty?

_____

_____

In what ways did Nehemiah seek to challenge and change the
situation at a structural/systemic level?

_____

_____

Can you think of other biblical characters that found themselves in positions of responsibility and were able to work toward structural change?

_____

_____

Why would Nehemiah be concerned about Israel's behavior being "mocked by enemy nations"?

_____

_____

In what ways did Nehemiah back up his working for systemic change with a change in his own personal lifestyle?

_____

_____

Why do you think this was important to him?

_____

_____

Lesson #3: Working for Change in Society

Nehemiah is an outstanding model of what the Bible teaches as a meaningful response to the poor. He doesn't hide behind his status, position, or wealth. Instead, he engages the poor at both the structural and personal level.

Wherever we find ourselves working—in government departments, political parties, nongovernmental organizations, municipal structures, multinational corporations, small businesses, health or education systems, or local neighborhoods—we too should seek to work for the welfare and prosperity of those we serve. At times this will mean challenging systems and structures that stand in the way of God's provision and prosperity for all people. This may require changing the priorities, structures, and processes of such organizations—particularly where they oppress or marginalize the vulnerable or the poor. Whether it be in advocating for fairer taxation systems, helping draft legislation against monopolistic or anti-competitive practices, or challenging the way employers and unions relate to each other in a particular industry, there are many opportunities for Christians to bring systemic change to the way provision and wealth are obtained.

 Food for Thought

Think about your own context (individually and collectively). What are some ways or opportunities you might have to work for justice?

_____

_____

_____

_____

Are there any specific examples from Nehemiah that would work in your sphere of influence?

_____

_____

_____

_____

"Teach Me to Love" Prayer

(Slightly adapted from Joy Cowley, *Aotearoa Psalms* [Pleroma, 2008])

> *Please God,*
>
> *I want to be a better lover.*
>
> *Where I come from, the meaning of that word is so distorted that it's more about taking than giving and I'm almost embarrassed to use it.*
>
> *But to become a better lover is what I need more than anything else.*
>
> *I want to love with the spontaneity of the small child, alive with delight.*
>
> *I want to love without discrimination, hugging everything you have created—earth, land, sunlight, shadows, brothers and sisters, and especially the stranger.*
>
> *I want to love recklessly with the kind of commitment that doesn't manufacture questions or balance giving against getting, but that takes a big step away from self-consciousness.*
>
> *I want to love with trust. There are fears in my life that are born of ignorance and that can be erased only by love itself.*
>
> *I know, dear God, that while my selfishness is always with me, love has a way of overcoming the obstacles to its fulfillment.*
>
> *So, please God, make me a better lover.*
>
> *I make this prayer in the name of the greatest lover (and giver) humanity has ever known, Jesus, who stretched out his arms to embrace the world and die for it.*
>
> *Amen.*

Chapter 9

Hope and Help in God's Provision

We have covered a lot of ground in this study series, which we will now seek to summarize and bring together in this final chapter. To do this we are going to focus on five elements that can characterize our approach to God's provision for our lives:

1. Trusting God for Provision

2. Resting Regularly

3. Working Diligently

4. Embracing the Effects of a Fallen World

5. Anticipating the Fully Restored Earth

Let's look briefly at each element.

Lesson #1: Trusting God for Provision

We are meant to depend on God for provision, meaning we should look to him to provide for us when our own means seem inadequate. The miracle of the feeding of the five thousand is a great example of this. God delights in making up what we lack. He is our provider. Jesus clearly tells us what God expects and wants us to ask him for what we need:

"Keep on asking, and you will receive what you ask for. Keep on seeking, and you will find. Keep on knocking, and the door will be opened to you. For everyone who asks, receives. Everyone who seeks, finds. And to everyone who knocks, the door will be opened. You parents—if your children ask for a loaf of bread, do you give them a stone instead? Or if they ask for a fish, do you give them a snake? Of course not! So if you sinful people know how to give good gifts to your children, how much more will your heavenly Father give good gifts to those who ask him." (Matthew 7:7–11)

The Apostle Paul also reminds us:

> And this same God who takes care of me will supply all your needs from his glorious riches, which have been given to us in Christ Jesus. (Philippians 4:19)

 Food for Thought

What is your biggest challenge in trusting that God will provide for you?

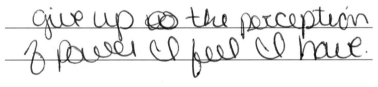

give up to the perception of power I feel I have.

How might those of us who are affluent be able to develop a genuine trust in God for our material needs, especially when we appear to have the means to be self-sufficient?

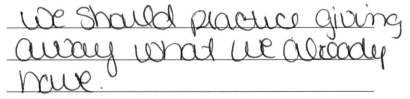

We should practice giving away what we already have.

Have you ever experienced God's provision in a totally unexpected way—or beyond what you really needed?

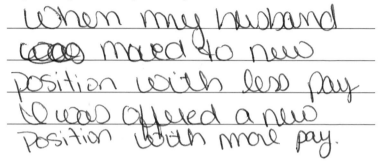

When my husband was moved to new position with less pay I was offered a new position with more pay.

Lesson #2: Resting Regularly

Another key way of trusting God for our provision is by developing a regular practice of rest. Sabbath is a repudiation of the drive for more. It reminds us that there is more to life than just producing and consuming, and who we are is not the sum total of our work or our bank accounts.

By resting, we must dare to trust God to provide for our needs (as the Israelites discovered in the wilderness), rather than working incessantly to provide for them ourselves. This is a challenge for those with compulsive work habits and those who struggle to put bread on the table. As writer and pastor Gordon MacDonald remarks in "Rest Stops" (*Life@Work Journal* 2, no.4):

> The more we want, the more revenue we must produce to get it. The more revenue we must produce, the longer and harder we work. So we build larger homes, buy more cars, take on added financial burdens and then find ourselves having to work harder to pay for it all. More work, less rest.

 *Food for Thought*

In what way/s do you agree or disagree with Gordon MacDonald's statement?

I completely agree the more money we have the more we feel we need & that requires more work to keep it up

What regular practice of rest/Sabbath do you have, and in what way does this help you to trust God for your provision?

I don't have a practice but I would like to start one.

Lesson #3: Working Diligently

Dependence on God is not a substitute for human labor. We are meant to work diligently and wisely. Although God is our provider, he calls us to use what we have in our hands, not what we don't have. As we observed in chapter 1 with Genesis 1–2, God's first gift to us for our provision is our ability to work. Even if disability, circumstances, or injustice make our work fall tragically short of meeting our needs, God begins by making use of what we *are* able to do. Then he makes up the difference from his inexhaustible riches.

> And this same God who takes care of me will supply all your needs from his glorious riches, which have been given to us in Christ Jesus. (Philippians 4:19)

 *Food for Thought*

Do you have circumstances in your life right now that keep you from being as productive as you would like? If so, think of ways that you can do whatever you can.

My shoulder has been bothering me lately so I have had a maid time sweeping. So I have traded chores with my husband

What might be some of the challenges for people working in your faith community?

Health + physical issues along with weather can be problems

Lesson #4: Embracing the Effects of a Fallen World

> Even while we were with you, we gave you this command: "Those unwilling to work will not get to eat." Yet we hear that some of you are living idle lives, refusing to work and meddling in other people's business. We command such people and urge them in the name of the Lord Jesus Christ to settle down and work to earn their own living. (2 Thessalonians 3:10–12)

Paul's approach is quite simple: No work, no eat. It does not matter whether it is paid or unpaid work. If there is useful work we can do, we cannot sit idle and expect God to bless our idleness. This means that even those who struggle to find or undertake paid work can still work in voluntary capacities. It is our responsibility to work to the degree we are able, and God's responsibility to ensure our needs are met.

Nowhere in Scripture does God promise that his followers will escape the effects of the fallen world. Paul certainly understood this:

> I have worked hard and long, enduring many sleepless nights. I have been hungry and thirsty and have often gone without food. I have shivered in the cold, without enough clothing to keep me warm. (2 Corinthians 11:27)

 Food for Thought

In other letters Paul suggests that God has always provided for him. How do you think he would reconcile this with his statements here about doing *without*?

Paul was given enough to be uncomfortable but not dangerous.

Can you think of other faithful biblical characters who also endured periods of time where circumstances, suffering, and persecution robbed them of what they needed materially?

Daniel in the lions chains

If God does not exempt us from the sufferings of the world, what *does* he promise to do for us?

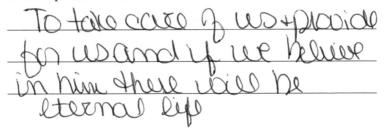

To take care of us + provide for us and if we believe in him there will be eternal life

Lesson #5: Anticipating the Fully Restored Earth

The Lord, through the prophet Isaiah, spoke hope to the Israelites centuries ago and speaks hope to us today as we anticipate a fully restored creation:

> "Look! I am creating new heavens and a new earth, and no one will even think about the old ones anymore. . . . In those days people will live in the houses they build and eat the fruit of their own vineyards. Unlike the past, invaders will not take their houses and confiscate their vineyards. For my people will live as long as trees, and my chosen ones will have time to enjoy their hard-won gains. They will not work in vain, and their children will not be doomed to misfortune. For they are people blessed by the Lord, and their children, too, will be blessed. . . . I will give Jerusalem a river of peace and prosperity. The wealth of the nations will flow to her."
> (Isaiah 65:17, 21–23; 66:12)

 Food for Thought

What does this passage indicate about the relationship between work and provision/blessing?

Even in the new heaven + Earth we will work but not in vain. He provide for us.

Isaiah paints the future in pictures that his audience could relate to. If he wrote this today using modern examples, how might he describe this final hope?

Everyone will have beautiful homes and food + we will not work constantly to get things what we need. We will be at peace.

Can you think of other parts of Scripture that give an indication of what the completion of God's redemption will look like for our provision?

In Rev 21-22 it tells us that we will feel at one with God and he will provide life along with an amazing landscape.

Summary

The final hope of Christians is to participate in the abundant, blessed life promised when the world is fully restored upon Christ's return. In the new earth there will be plenty for all. No one will lack provision. Justice will reign. Wealth will be experienced by everyone, without corrupting any person or anything. All will be as God always intended it to be.

Final Reflections

Food for Thought

Share something from these studies you have found particularly challenging or surprising.

The idea that God has put us incharge of the money we earn, but it belongs to him.

Share one specific change you intend to make as a result of these studies.

I will work harder to spend money & time helping others.

Prayer

(Adapted from "We Are World Christians!" by Gordon Aeschliman)

Lord,

You tell us to seek first your kingdom. Then you will meet our needs. . . .

So we ask you, don't give us blessings—give us grace to be unquestionably obedient to your every last command and desire.

Don't give us status—give us a place to serve.

Don't give us things for our use—use us.

Don't give us a mansion to live in—give us a springboard to take Christ's love to the whole world.

Don't give us good jobs—put us to work.

Don't give us comfort—command us.

Don't give us pleasure—give us perspective.

Don't give us entertainment—enable us.

Don't give us good salaries—give us strength to do your will.

We want our great joy in life to be found in pleasing you, O Lord—and for there to be no other joy comparable. . . .

We don't want to seek our personal rights—we want to see all people set free. . . .

We don't want to give ten percent of our income to you—we want to give it all.

We don't work for you from 8–5—we are yours for 24 hours of each day. . . .

We don't want to take pride in acquiring things—no, hoarding shames us.

We acknowledge that it is senseless to talk of availability or willingness, if we are not actively obeying you and serving others.

Help us to make this prayer a reality.

Amen.

Wisdom for Using This Study in the Workplace

Community within the workplace is a good thing, and a Christian community within the workplace is even better. Sensitivity is needed, however, when we get together in the workplace (even a Christian workplace) to enjoy fellowship time together, learn what the Bible has to say about our work, and encourage one another in Jesus' name. When you meet at your place of employment, here are some guidelines to keep in mind:

- Be sensitive to your surroundings. Know your company policy about having such a group on company property. Make sure not to give the impression that this is a secret or exclusive group.

- Be sensitive to time constraints. Don't go over your allotted time. Don't be late to work! Make sure you are a good witness to the others (especially non-Christians) in your workplace by being fully committed to your work during working hours and doing all your work with excellence.

- Be sensitive to the shy or silent members of your group. Encourage everyone in the group and give them a chance to talk.

- Be sensitive to the others by being prepared. Read the Bible study material and Scripture passages and think about your answers to the questions ahead of time.

These Bible studies are based on the Theology of Work biblical commentary. Besides reading the commentary, please visit the Theology of Work website (www.theologyofwork.org) for videos, interviews, and other material on the Bible and your work.

Leader's Guide

Living Word. It is always exciting to start a new group and study. The possibilities of growth and relationship are limitless when we engage with one another and with God's word. Always remember that God's word is "alive and active, sharper than any double-edged sword" (Heb. 4:12) and when you study his word, it should change you.

A Way Has Been Made. Please know you and each person joining your study have been prayed for by people you will probably never meet who share your faith. And remember that "the LORD himself goes before you and will be with you; he will never leave you nor forsake you. Do not be afraid; do not be discouraged" (Deut. 31:8). As a leader, you need to know that truth. Remind yourself of it throughout this study.

Pray. It is always a good idea to pray for your study and those involved weeks before you even begin. It is recommended to pray for yourself as leader, your group members, and the time you are about to spend together. It's no small thing you are about to start and the more you prepare in the Spirit, the better. Apart from Jesus, we can do nothing (John 14:5). Remain in him and "you will bear much fruit" (John 15:5). It's also a good idea to have trusted friends pray and intercede for you and your group as you work through the study.

Spiritual Battle. Like it or not, the Bible teaches that we are in the middle of a spiritual battle. The enemy would like nothing more than for this study to be ineffective. It would be part of his scheme to have group members not show up or engage in any discussion. His victory would be that your group just passes time together going through the motions of a yet another Bible study. You, as a leader, are a threat to the enemy, as it is your desire to lead people down the path of righteousness (as taught in Proverbs). Read Ephesians 6:10–20 and put your armor on.

Scripture. Prepare before your study by reading the selected Scripture verses ahead of time.

Chapters. Each chapter contains approximately three lessons. As you work through the lessons, keep in mind the particular chapter theme in connection with the lessons. These lessons are designed so that you can go through them in thirty minutes each.

Lessons. Each lesson has teaching points with their own discussion questions. This format should keep the participants engaged with the text and one another.

Food for Thought. The questions at the end of the teaching points are there to create discussion and deepen the connection between each person and the content being addressed. You know the people in your group and should feel free to come up with your own questions or adapt the ones provided to best meet the needs of your group. Again, this would require some preparation beforehand.

Opening and Closing Prayers. Sometimes prayer prompts are given before and usually after each lesson. These are just suggestions. You know your group and the needs present, so please feel free to pray accordingly.

Bible Commentary. The Theology of Work series contains a variety of books to help you apply the Scriptures and Christian faith to your work. This Bible study is based on the *Theology of Work Bible Commentary*, examining what the Bible say about work. This commentary is intended to assist those with theological training or interest to conduct in-depth research into passages or books of Scripture.

Video Clips. The Theology of Work website (www.theologyofwork .org) provides good video footage of people from the marketplace highlighting the teaching from all the books of the Bible. It would be great to incorporate some of these videos into your teaching time.

Enjoy your study! Remember that God's word does not return void—ever. It produces fruit and succeeds in whatever way God has intended it to succeed.

> "So shall my word be that goes out from my mouth;
>   it shall not return to me empty,
>   but it shall accomplish that which I purpose,
>   and shall succeed in the thing for which I sent it." (Isa. 55:11)

Explore what the Bible has to say about work, book by book.

THE BIBLE AND YOUR WORK
Study Series

HENDRICKSON PUBLISHERS

THEOLOGY OF WORK   PROJECT